MW01222352

TOTEMS

An Easy to Read Handbook On:

Animal Guides, Protectors, Totems& Power Animals©

By: Chantal M. Cash; CH, RMT

Table of Contents

Introduction

For those interested in Shamanism, Energy Healing or simply love animals this is the book for you. Most people on this planet love animals. We cherish nature and many of us find solace in animals; especially our pets. Think back now on your childhood. What was your favorite past time? I know for me, my Grandmother had no pets but she would send us to a Farm down a few miles from where she lived. They had house cats, barn cats, dogs, chickens, pigs and cows. I think they even had one horse. It was a Tom Girl's dream. Tree climber and hugger: from my youth. Growing up, when I later moved to a new city my Dad was a lover of cats and so we got three, and he many years later also got two Shepherd/collie mix dogs.

Besides the domesticated cat, my first true encounter with one of my animal totems was when I was about 15 years old. I was a very unhappy teenager. Really had many difficult times and several traumas to digest as well. Not knowing how to swim was partly due to an almost accidental drowning when I was a small child.

So when this group asked me to go up to The Boundary Waters National Park I was very reluctant. In fact, I was quite fearful due to my previous drowning experience.

I decided to go, and it was a ten day trip. We would go day by day in our canoes taking our canoes through ports and basically living outside in tents, and being outside rain or shine; exposed to nature and the elements. It was close to the end of our journey and my group we decided to check out an Island. This island was close to where a woman had reportedly lived for many years and was supposed to be the last person allowed to live on the land. We were on an island across from that cabin where the old woman once lived.

We were planning on staying on this island as it was a perfect site to land and set up camp. We began to explore and decided to look for the outhouse. There were seven of us girls, and though I could not swim I was a proficient hiker and loved to explore. I took the lead to search for the toilet. We got about a half of a mile and we smelled this horrible smell. It was a stench like rotten meat or like something had died. We kept going and heard a loud crash in the woods and in the brush.

Within moments of that sound a very large black bear came lumbering out of the woods. We stood there, somewhat frightful. I remember the bear approached us, but I was the closest to him. He stood up then on his back two legs and made this funny grumbling sound. The girls behind me began to scream and they ran, of course, leaving me there to face the bear alone.

I did not move. I was scared, but I stood there looking at the Bear, about four times my size. He was immense and I knew he could kill me with one swipe of a paw. I did not breathe, I did not pray, I did not blink. I simply smiled and said, "Hello." He waved his paw up in the air, like he too was saying hello. He grumbled a few moans and he got back down and wandered down into the woods heading towards a secluded beach on the other side of the island.

I will never forget that bear. I cannot forget how he smelled, and looked and the sounds he made. I believe looking back now; it was a totem or a protector animal. For me, the Bear stands for leadership; it is funny to point out too: that I was at the front of the line. I am sure this too is representative in other cultures and their animal guides. So, there is a reason, a season, and a lifetime for every person, animal, plant or consciousness; and: for every "ENERGY" that exists in our world here and in our Universe, and abroad.

Animals are so important to humans. I do not feel that we could co-exist without them. The plants, animals, sea creatures, the birds, and any other creeping thing: all of these species have a purpose and a meaning for their existence. This book will describe in detail the varying opinions on Animal Guides and Totems. We will go into the difference between a Power Animal and a Totem, for instance. There are many viewpoints on this matter. While I will go into some other professional viewpoints on this matter; most of this is strictly opinion, and should be viewed as such.

Think now on any animal that moves your spirit. How do these creatures great and small make you feel inside? Do you enjoy one animal over another? Are there some that cause you to be afraid? Do you prefer flying things over creeping things? Can you stomach insects such as cockroaches or spiders crawling on you? Is there an animal that would otherwise be harmful, that for you makes you feel good or allows you to be close to them? Do you like snakes or despise them? These are questions you should ask yourself when trying to acquaint yourself with any animal.

An example would be my story about the bear. I have seen people hold venomous snakes, or scorpions. I have seen bees land on folk's and never sting them. There are many ways to detect (in your environment alone) which animals are right for you and in many cases assigned to you like a protector. The above mentioned questions are often a way to notice what our animal totems might be. Or even what animals we should be paying attention to. If you get stung by a bee, well that insect/animal wants you to pay attention and there is probably a lesson in it or some message that they are trying to bring you.

So let us go and explore the world of animals and their secret meanings. Think of how unique each one of us human beings are. The animal kingdom: is an extra ordinary exception. With the vast array of species and the many different kinds, of beasts, fowl, and other animals; it is truly awesome to think about! The possibilities seem endless, and in fact, are quite close. Their meanings, are descriptive and often reflect our personalities . The only thing here to fear from the animals is: our-selves. Our fears often get in the way of truth and in understanding it. The natural kingdom is misunderstood, so let us begin to understand.

Please note that there are some citations and direct quotes in this text. However, much of the work is my own personal translation of the animals and their hidden meanings but also based on studying animals and their personalities. Not everything may be viewed in the same way—so believe that this is my truest interpretation of these animals, Some viewpoints as I wrote this text and did my research became evident were the same as others.

What are Animal Totems, Spirit Guides and Protectors?

Ancient lore is what makes up many of our legends and stories throughout our human history. It is hard to know what happened before mankind began to document through either pictographs, etchings and eventually wrote on stone tablets to describe what they were seeing, hearing and feeling. Animals have been found to be in these pictographs and also have been used as characters in stories for as long as man has spoken and told tales of valor and triumph either through their own actions or by observing animals; they have expressed themselves even as heroes in the guise of an animal, bird or some other type of creature.

Animals in many ways were objects for us to wonder about. Humans before they became what they are now, I feel had little understanding of the way the world worked much less how our planet, galaxies and solar system worked. Animals have been symbols to human beings for eons of ages on this planet and their existence is crucial to our human survival. Not only do we use them for food, warmth, and even shelter in some cases; they have been burning symbols of freedom, happiness, and love in the hearts of humanity since the dawn of time.

Many cultures and belief systems have some idea of animals and what they are often used for: specifically, how society viewed them. Some animals like wolves have often been vilified. Other animals like Deer are often sought after for their antlers. Elephants are still hunted today for their tusks despite protests of animal rights activists. There are so many animals and each to their own: they have a story to tell. They have offspring. Do they love their kin the way we do? What do you think? They are vibrant, they have lives and make their impact on the world the same as you or I do. Why do we really treat them so differently? Mostly due to fear, and our cultural programming, this is the truth of the matter.

There are four general types of Cultural viewpoints that I will address in this short book that pertain to animals and their symbolism: Animal Spirit Guides, Animal Protectors, Animal Totems, and Power Animals. When I am referring to cultural viewpoints it means I am taking concepts from different cultures who utilize these ideas in their daily lives and in their spiritual visions, many of these traditions go back hundreds of thousands of years or more. These stories and traditions are very real to the people who tell them. The people used to understand the animals and had more respect for their secular wisdom compared to some of the folks of today, but the remnants of those old stories still exist, and some places rely on those stories to keep their own inner wisdom burning along with communal wisdom.

The three traditions that enhanced my viewpoints are: Druidic tradition, Native American or Shamanic and of course my personal favorite the Chinese Astrology system. While in any of the three belief systems these three ideas as mentioned above can all be incorporated into each their own. However to make this seem more logical and with this viewpoint in mind I will be dividing them into these three categories. The fourth category Power Animal is for me—a more modern term and will be talked about in further length, shortly.

I feel that Animal Totems often pertain to Shamanic or Native American traditions. I will go into further details in a moment. I would lean also towards: in Chinese Astrology that the animals are more like Protectors, specifically regarding your birth sign animal. It is often a representation of ones personality in this lifetime, in my opinion. Thirdly, in regards to Druidic or Wiccan traditions they often leaned on animals to carry messages and receive messages back. I am leaning towards using the term Animal Spirit Guide to describe the Druid concept.

In regards to Power Animals this is often a term used in more New Age circles. It is exactly what the term means: Power combined with Animal makes for a strong combination. Many folks I know use this term and this is very acceptable among today's Metaphysical discussion groups.

As I stated even though these terms could be interchangeable, I have chosen to put them in this category just for compartmentalizing purposes. You can call your animal guides whatever you like. I myself interchange between all four terms. I simply wish to help the mind absorb in layman's terms what these actual concepts mean and typically where they originated from.

This is my own personal opinion and much of my past and present beliefs are reflected in my work with animals. I was raised around Native American people as my father's partner of 17 years was full blooded Lakota Sioux. I practiced for a short while certain aspects of Buddhism and relied heavily on the wisdom of some monks, the Lam Rim and Chinese Astrology and the defining nature of the personalities of these people has been revealed to me; and many folks—their personalities reflect those traits of their assigned animal protectors and their birth totems.

As I grew older I became interested in Druidism and also Shamanism. Eventually I was drawn closer to Shamanism, but still I learned about these three cultures and incorporated their spiritual ideas into my work. I especially was drawn to their ideas on animals and what they thought about their significance and purpose. There were differences and similarities, of course, and some of these will be reflected in the course of this book.

Eventually, I learned to draw from these animals in my own way and through my own ideas and personal reflections. Of course this led me to better understand animals and their functions outside of the obvious purpose that many people see animals as being only a food source, or a sport to hunt, let us say. I believe that eventually, our future will lead us to NOT eating animals. I feel that in the beginning before this "fall" animals and humans and other beings co-existed harmoniously without ever thinking of consuming one another. With that said, since that time we have all been guilty of this, and having known no other way we simply think that this is what we will always be doing.

Animal Protectors

So let us move now onto these four categories beginning with Animal Protectors. In Chinese lore there are 12 animals, same as in the Greek astrology signs. However, respectively in Chinese lore these animals all represent a year and also an element. The twelve animals are as follows: Rat, Ox, Tiger, Rabbit, Dragon, Snake, Horse, Goat, Monkey, Rooster, Dog, and Pig. In addition, to having these twelve animals there are "inner animals" that go by the Month. Also *Day Animals* are referred to as "true animals" and *Animals for the Hours* are known as "secret animals". We will not be exploring that complex topic in this text as that would make for a whole other book in and of itself (Wikipedia, 6/14/2013).

My focus here is not the semantics of astrology it is to direct our attention to the animals themselves. I was born in 1971 and that makes me a Boar or a Pig. We are fun loving, brutally honest and we make lifelong friends; the snake is my nemesis. Now in regards to Animal Protectors know that your birth animal is one of your Protectors, regardless of what your belief system is. You will either have an intense like or dislike for that animal. Most people know what their Chinese Zodiac sign is so it is already a part of their consciousness. Two of my best friends were snakes. Oh, the relationship at first was very good. Snakes though tend to want to control the pig, however, when the Pig is thwarted or feels in jeopardy the PIG will trample anything that is under foot. The Pig is so sensitive that often their feelings become hurt easily through negative words and actions of other people. They often will walk away from friendships if the same amount of affection is not equally given. This is just an example. So I will go through in short each of the animal's signs and you may apply it if you wish to your ideas about this type of Animal Protector.

If you do not know what your Chinese Zodiac sign is you can easily find out by entering the year you were born into an internet search engine: keyword Chinese animal sign—and then you will know. It is very interesting to study these animals and their personal traits—you will find much of it to be true!

The Chinese Zodiac Animals

Rat: Just like a rat; yes these folks with this disposition they are very clever and cunning. They are sharp as tacks. They also are more inclined towards materialism and really like money. They can be greedy, but they are knowledge seekers. This animal is compatible with Dragon or Monkey.

Ox: Just as an Ox is big and sturdy this person is like that, if not in appearance than in behavior. They are often in a position to take a leadership role. They are stubborn and quite serious. The Ox is compatible with Snake or Rooster. They are protective and a very good friend or companion to have.

Tiger: Like the Ox they have a strong leader ship quality about them. Like a Tiger though they are ready to pounce at any time. They can be moody, eccentric and sometimes egotistical. Often courageous and ambitious they do not look back when making a decision. The Tiger is compatible with the Horse or a Dog.

Rabbit: The rabbit is considered timid by nature. These people who bare this sign are very compassionate and are also sincere. They can be easily taken advantage of by others, who find them to be a pushover. These folks are most compatible with the Pig and the Goat.

Dragon: The Dragon is an extremely powerful sign and persons under this sign are extremely enigmatic. They are often lucky at love and are quite arrogant at times. They often do what they must to stay on top of their own world. Often motivated by their own inner fire, the Dragon is creative but also can be aggressive. The Dragon is compatible with Monkey and the Rat.

Snake: The Snake is analytical, charming, introverted and they are very cunning. They can be prone to jealousy and often are extremely intelligent. They can be quite silky in their seductions. If a snake is wronged, he will find a way to get even; it is just a part of their nature. They are most compatible with Ox and Rooster.

Horse: The Horse is an animal that was supposed to remain free. These people with this trait are in love with traveling. They enjoy love and intimacy. They are very sharp witted, and can be quite impatient. The horse is compatible with the Dog or a Tiger.

Goat: Many Goat people like to be alone and are often great thinkers. They are creative. They can be high-strung and prone to anxiety. They are also unorganized. They are better at thinking than doing. They need lots of support and reassurance. Appearance is important to them and they are compatible with Pig and Rabbit.

Monkey: The Monkey is a good listener. They enjoy having fun above all else. Prone to slight selfishness, they please themselves before others. They have weak morals and they are not good in long term relationships. This is the one sign that can overrule the snake, all other signs are prone to fall to the snakes charms. Not the monkey, of course. The monkey is compatible with the Rat or Dragon.

Rooster: The Rooster is practical and quite resourceful. They are very honest and straightforward in their approaches with others. They are prone to perfectionism. They like to "strut" their stuff, not arrogantly though. They want others to know their accomplishments. They are most compatible with the Snake and the Ox.

Dog: Many of us associate the Dog with loyalty and this is the case with this idea of a dog and its personality. They are faithful and can be honest about important things but they are also quite prone to telling white lies. They are easily overwhelmed and are quite moody. They are also quite sensitive individuals at times. They are compatible with the Tiger or the Horse.

Pig: Finally, the Pig is good natured and has good taste in many things. They do like the finer things in life but they are never rude and therefore not considered snobbish. They make great companions and are always smiling and nice. They make lifelong friends, but have few. If, you cross them however, beware! They can go from cute pig to wild boar, if pushed to the limits. Constant knowledge seekers and quite intelligent, they are unique in each their own personality. They are most compatible with Rabbit or the Goat.

Note to readers: All animals and dates and other information for the Chinese Astrology section were retrieved from: www.chinesezodiac.com/signs. There are many sites on this subject and books too. If you want to know more do some of your own research.

This concludes the explanation of each animal and their individual traits, in short. These examples are merely used to explain these common traits of the animals and observation proves that humans born in their respective year: share in these traits presented by this form of astrological philosophy.

So when someone says, "So and so, is so snaky." Chances are they really are snaky because they were born in The Year of the Snake. For those who are interested in this type of animal protector it is best to get to know this system and learn about the animals and which ones are compatible with your sign. I have found this form of working with the animals and their sign's very effective and can enhance any friendship or relationship, when you abide by the laws of these concepts and acknowledge certain traditions, the animals begin to work together harmoniously and I discovered that my friendships became easier once I understood the ideas that he animals wished to convey.

Figure 1: Animal Power Shield by AHONU

This is an example of an Animal Power Shield by Master Spirit Artist: AHONU. This is my son William's shield. There are four cats. The wing represents the Griffin for his mystical totem. In addition there are four stags which represent my son's Welsh ancestry. There are sixteen elephants and what looks like barrels of monkey's to remind us to stay young at heart. The keywords for each animal would be: Cat-mystery, Griffin Protection, Baboon—Great Thinker and Writer, Stag—Independence and finally—the elephant—ancient wisdom. See www.AHONU.com to see his interpretation of this beautiful masterpiece.

Animal Spirit Guides

The next category we will be focusing on is Animal Spirit Guides. I will be using Druidic philosophy here and a tool I use is *The Druid Animal Oracle.* Every culture has their own take on animals and what they mean to them as a culture. I do give animal totem/and animal spirit guide readings. I use this deck to give people a chance to learn from those particular cultures and their ancient animal wisdom: be it Druid or Native American perspective. Some people still get that reading and they connect with those animals in a different manner. There is no right or wrong way to get an animal totem reading.

Celtic tradition breeds great reverence for animals. Phillip and Stephanie Carr-Gomm do a remarkable and beautiful depiction of each animal. Stories are given to enhance the reader and the receiver's interpretation of these animals. Their great wisdom is highly reflective and the images are also enchanting. I actually own all three decks: Druid Tarot, Animal Oracle, and Plant Oracle Medicine, also.

I will not go into every animal that they have a card and an explanation for. This deck is a tool of divination for those who wish to be taught by the Animals, I highly recommend this deck. The Celt's viewed their animals as Teachers, and in some cases was even reflected in their stories and tales as The Elders often told them.

There were clans and tribes, same as in the Native American way of life. The ancestors of these people really reveled in their beliefs regarding animals. Their names often depicted as such, (even reflecting in some family names today), like FOX, (Carr-Gomm, page 6-7). These people who were part of a clan or tribe often bore many resemblances even to the animal their family was said to have originated from. These families also used Totems as described in Native American lore.

Many of these people in death chose to be buried with certain animals. In addition, they wore their teeth, claws, and bones as charms and considered them treasures. They too, like Native American peoples used all the parts of the animal not allowing any part of it to go to waste. The concept though similar, Druid wisdom revered the Goddess and she must be appeased; one must ask for permission to take any animal's life in the forest first, otherwise it was believed that there were swift and sure consequences to follow.

Make no mistake: this reverence for animals has always been there. As teachers they do remain older than us humans, we should value them not only as teachers but also as a Source of Life and Power. As noted in my introduction, the Bear came to me in this life, but he/she has come to many others in rage or in peace and in a similar fashion.

As noted by Carr-Gomm there are alters that date back about 70,000 years ago in Switzerland honoring the sacredness of the bear. In addition, they said in France about 19,000 years ago they found caves that had ceremonial depictions of bears as well. Human beings have always been impressed with power and strength. The Bear is an excellent example of such an animal. Kings wanted to be Bear like so that their enemies would fear them and their subjects would respect them (Carr-Gomm, Page. 7).

Druids and other Celtic peoples used the animal skins, antlers, their heads even to become one with the animal and gain some of their essence. By today's standards much of this seems brutal and out of date, but many cultures still adhere to old beliefs and cultural philosophies, to ensure that their way of life does not die. They use these parts of the animals to truly "become" as close to that animal as possible. So with these practices, it is noted that many animals were sacrificed and buried, and in ritual fashion I might add (Carr-Gomm, page 8).

We will go into greater detail about Shamanism, but in their Introduction they do say that it is liken to that, and there are many Shamanic ideas that have been interwoven into the Druid philosophy. It merely is a different language, and a different part of the world; but it still has a similar theme and format. So, some of these terms will be interchangeable between Druid ideas and Native American ones, and still yet may find some similarities connecting things to the Chinese system as well. I do find similar themes in many cultures; including Africa which is described towards the end of this book. As I said my main focus is the animals, not so much the culture and belief system. It merely shows that some animals are only living in a certain part of the world.

Similar to what was explained in the Chinese Astrology section above, Druid tradition also has Inner Animals, Power Animals and Totem Guides. So again, these are broad range terms I merely want individuals to see though similar, they each have their own traditions and ideas in regards to the traits of any animal. Animals are symbols; they can either empower us with awe or they can capture us with fear and enslave us. A Bear for some could represent strength and courage and yet to another person, it might strike pure fear in them.

Here is an example. When I was young I fell into a hornets nest. I got stung several times. I was very afraid for so long of any insect that buzzed, looked like it might sting, and any type of flying insect. I was terrified. Now many years later I understand that insect was trying to help me by confronting me with my own terror. Now bees and wasps stay away from me. We co-exist without thinking too much about the other. I know they are my allies now and not my enemy. I never swat at them anymore, and I give them absolute respect. We will go into it shortly some examples of Druid animals and their strengths for the person who wishes to access their power and energy.

Inner animals are simply the ones we dream about according to Carr-Gomm. They are aspects of our psyche and we often do not even understand what we see in dreams. These inner animals have much to teach and they help to enhance our "inner world," and allows us to explore unchartered realms. Secondly, Power Animal: though I often use this term when speaking to New Age groups and individuals, the Druid and Native American traditions also utilizes this term. A Power Animal is an animal in spirit form, behind the veil. It is there and often chooses us; it will give energy, healing, and much like a Muse will give us inspiring thoughts. Because these Power animals carry a certain frequency and knowledge it is considered a form of medicine and should be viewed as such.

Third, as in Native tradition they too use the term Totem, however, for this we will call it a Familiar. We will use this term so as not to get the two philosophies confused. This familiar or "totem" so you know, you will be much more aware of their presence. They too are guides, teachers, and can even become our friends.

The reason that many of us have issues with certain animals is that we are rejecting that presence or connection. If we allow our fear of animals to take over, and many of them are unnatural. I am not saying go and pet a BEAR or a LION: never approach a wild animal. That is never wise. I am saying to meditate on your animals that come and seek you out. Animals come to me all the time. I have had a fox come and visit me quite often. I know that the fox is one of my animal spirit guides. When he comes to visit, literally, I talk to him and he sits for a few moments and then he moves on. As a result from these connections you may even find that you can communicate with animals mentally. That of course, is an entire chapter all by itself, though will not be any subject in this book.

Animal Spirit Guides

I will not go into every animal in Celtic tradition but I will discuss the ones I feel that have the most significant baring on their history and the ones I feel connected to the most. In The Druid Animal Oracle book they have thirty-three animals noted. I am going to focus on twelve animals for this section, as in the Chinese Zodiac signs.

Below are some listed animals and their respective key words. All keywords are a direct quote from Philip and Stephanie's Oracle book that I use particularly in some of my readings. This is one of the best examples, (in my opinion) of Druid tradition so I will be using this as my only example.

BEAR: Primal Power, Sovereignty, Intuition combined with Instinct.

BEE: Community, Celebration and Organization.

CAT: Guardianship, Detachment and Sensuality.

Eagle: Courage, Intelligence, and Renewal.

Fox: Diplomacy, Cunning, and Wildness.

Frog: Sensitivity, Medicine, Beauty and Power that is hidden.

Hawk: Cleansing, Nobility, and Recollection.

Horse: The Goddess, The Land and Travel.

Raven: Healing, Initiation and Protection.

Stag: Independence, Pride, and Purification.

Swan: Beauty, Love and the Soul.

Wolf: Intuition, Learning and The Shadow Self.

The Bear

So, we will begin with Bear and work our way through every animal that is listed. We have touched a little bit on the greatness of the Bear. This animal is the subject of many stories, conquests and triumphs. There are many depictions of Kings and Clan leaders using their hide and head as part of their wardrobe. This was done to show their power and their prestige. The Bear in these departments is like the equivalence of the Lion in the jungle. This animal reigns supreme in these here parts. It is the Beast of Beasts!

I will go into later an interpretation of my own with certain animals, the Bear would be included. The Bear is like they say in their book a very instinctual animal. In cold weather it hibernates. Its nose knows where to take him. The heart of a Bear is like that of a sovereign nation. This animal was adopted by people of supreme or high authority. It definitely commands attention and respect.

The Bee

The Bee is resilient. It speaks about community and harmony inside of any given community. According to Philip and Stephanie "The Bee in the Druid tradition comes from a Paradise world of The Sun and The Spirit" (Carr-Gomm, Page. 110) A sacred drink known to the Druids was called Mead, and honey was a key ingredient. So Bees were very sacred to them. So not only did the Druids consider the honey a gift from the Bee's they also looked at the wax as an asset. Britain was known as The Island of Honey" and in Ireland bees and their hives were protected and it was a capital crime to steal bees (Carr-Gomm, Page. 113).

The term "Queen Bee" for anyone would likely be interpreted as a Goddess symbol. As such, this is how the Bee was interpreted. The bee acts on behalf of the entire hive to serve the Queen. They hum and buzz content with their miniscule tasks that they do; and they give constant adoration to their Queen. They live for her, but not once do they falter and work tirelessly to keep their community thriving. Nothing seems to keep them from their tasks. They are all about focus and attention.

The Cat

The Cat is one of my favorite domesticated animals. It is representative of mystery and finding answers to those mysteries. Cats are for the most part independent animals in their own right. Anyone who has a cat knows that they most often prefer their own company. In the Druid tradition it is very important to note how important this animal actually is. Many tribes and clans used this animal to depict the traits that they wanted others to see in themselves. They demand respect and attention. Often curious—sometimes this leads the cat into trouble or tight places. Though she does represent sensuality but she is very proud and affection is given and received on his or her own terms. I feel that the cat is mysterious and they do have distinct personalities and in some cases, even egos. The cat is sacred and impressive to these people.

The Eagle

Originally I was going to choose the Dog to fill this spot, but Dog is loyal and that is a similar theme running through many cultures. So we shall focus on the Eagle. This bird with its vast wingspan and its remarkable appearance is truly a sight to behold. Back in the times of Arthurian legend the Eagle was a symbol of the guardians that watched over King Arthur's body. In addition, according to the *Druid Oracle Book*: the Eagle was said to influence the weather. Not only the Druids, but also the Scots and the Welsh saw Eagles as one of their sacred shape-shifting animals.

The Eagle is a symbol of rejuvenation. This amazing bird will bring you confidence and courage. The Eagle soars through the air without any cares or worries; it compels you to do the same. This bird also gives us the courage to take risks, and it is considered an art of plunging. Go for it, is what it is essentially saying. According to Philip and Stephanie in their book there is an Irish tradition that states that Adam and Eve are alive and living as Eagles. The Eagle though it seems detached-- it sticks its face right in the heart of the lake itself. They dive right in. It suggests you do the same with your emotions, and "enjoy those depths of feeling; knowledge is thus transformed into wisdom" (Carr-Gomm, Page. 84).

Fox

The fox is one of my favorite animals. I can see why The Druids considered this animal in matters of some importance. Like watching the Fox inspect the ice in a spring thaw to see if it is safe. How smart this animal is. I have been fortunate this year to have seen two or three different foxes. They have come to my home and sat under my pine tree. I also have Foxglove growing in the front. So I wondered if there was some connection, as he showed up after I planted it.

So, Fox in Celtic and Druid tradition is a very strong Animal to have on your side. To be the Son of a Fox meant "Strong in Counsel." It is important to note that the Celts often did look at the positive traits more than the negative ones. In addition, the Celt's did hunt the fox for sport, but mainly it was used for bedding and clothing. It was indeed a highly prized type of fur to own. Yes, the fox is cunning and sly. Often they wait in the shadows observing waiting for their opportune moment to arrive. Do they hold a pearl of wisdom in their mouth that we still do not understand?

Finally, they are wild. I have watched them by my home, and they truly are wild. They also seem to be loners and wanderers, yet, content with themselves— that they are. In addition, the Fox is the keeper of the fairy realm and he can help you see behind the veil. It may even be a sign that you need to be observant and remain hidden until you are supposed to be seen.

(Side note: it is 6/16/2013 and I was literally proof reading the Fox section when I casually looked outside to see a Fox sitting outside of my window eating some bread on the ground. I spoke to it for a while and I took this picture. Need I say more?

Figure 3: Young Fox in my front yard on 6/16/2013 around 9:00pm.

Frog

There is nothing like a warm summer evening and listening to the croaking of the frogs. Their rhythm and singing calms the senses. It is no wonder that the Frog is one of the Druid's sacred animals. Look into the wise old eyes of a Frog. There often is no way of telling how old he or she is. It is imperative: the Oracle is saying that even though something might appear ugly, there is great beauty in all things. You must look behind the appearance of someone or something and embrace that beautiful magic despite what their appearance might be (Carr-Gomm, Page. 64-65).

Think of stories that involve frogs. There are fairy tales of course, but Carr-Gomm's book describes this theme well. Movies have even shown this Frog Prince such as *Shrek.* The Frog Prince is an overall theme, in Celtic lore, but in general the frog is a great animal spirit to have on your side. They will carry you through treacherous waters knowing how to navigate through those murky waters; jumping from lily pad to lily pad. Frog Medicine is powerful and is considered a Familiar for those who may consider practicing White Magic this option is better than what they once did: they used Frogs in their potions; witches often did. So Frogs were often associated with the occult—but it truly represents healing and the blessings that water can bring.

Figure 4: This is a Frog I drew out of chalk.

Hawk

I am part Welsh. My Celtic permanent totem is the Hawk—specifically the Red-Tailed Hawk. I consider this to be one of seven sacred birds. That we will go into at another time. The Hawk and other birds of prey have always been inspiring for many Shamans, Medicine Men and Women, and Sages. Imagine times long past when men and women used Falcons to carry messages to neighboring Kingdoms. Or these men of re-known they stood proud with their Hawks perched on their leather clad arms. Many of them were Lords of the Forests and they needed a bird to be their eyes in the sky. This was an old way.

Now according to the King Arthur legend, the King's nephew whose name traditionally was Gawain—in Welsh he was known as Gwalchmai; which is translated as The Hawk of May. This powerful bird is often a symbol of The Grail Quest. With this come words like—healing, initiation, and for many—completion (Carr-Gomm, Page. 44). The Hawk reminds us of reaching for our dreams, to embrace the dawn of a new day. Remember, it is considered a blessing for your day to see a hawk first thing in the morning. You should never point directly at a hawk for it is considered a sign of disrespect, (that is an old wives tale my Grandmother once told me).

Horse

The Horse is by far one of the most majestic creatures that have ever lived. The horse is a true symbol of the journey of the soul and the heart. This is another animal that truly represents the symbol of the Goddess. Whether it is traveling abroad or in the inner realms—the horse compels us to travel and she is the one who would provoke our journey—inward or outward. She invokes the word FREEDOM! She represents speed, energy and power.

In the Druid tradition the Horse Goddess is associated with the cycle of life and death. The horse is also closely connected to the Sun, and was imagined that a chariot pulled by horses carried the Goddess that streaked across the sky! The horse, no doubt is truly an impeccable animal to have at your back.

Raven

I think that the key words that describe this crafty bird are perfect, though there is more to the Raven than what is described in _The Druid Animal Oracle._ Healing and Initiation seem to sometimes go hand in hand, so these key words are quite fitting for the Raven.

If this is your Guide, be aware that it is very protective of its charges. You may find if this is your animal that Raven's will follow you, or croak at you as if trying to speak. Many people fear these bold birds, but know that they are just exuding their power. Not only are they associated with healing they are also connected to those who induce prophetic vision and are considered a bird of prophecy and psychic vision. Also, Ravens are very intelligent and can even mimic human words. The Raven though used like a "familiar" it was a bird that could go into the inner worlds and retrieve crucial information for the seeker or the Shaman(Carr-Gomm, Page. 66-68).

Stag

In other cultures it is simply known as a Deer or a Buck. In this tradition it is called for a Male a Stag and a female is known as a Hind. In this tradition there is the God known as: Cerenunnos who has the body of a man and the head of a stag. Not only do the initial key words strike a chord: there is more…grace, majesty, and integrity around the words that are used by Philip and Stephanie when they discuss this animal in depth. There is much to say about this strong yet passive creature. This animal breeds dignity inside of us. It allows us to reach for independence. Though it was merely my opinion in regards to the Bear mentioned earlier, the Stag is considered The Lord of the Forest in many of the Celtic traditions. The antlers have a King like symbolism about them. In British tradition, it is also mentioned that the Stag is one of the five totem animals and thus is one among the five animals that marks a journey and carries us deeply into the insight of the Druids and the realms of the world behind the veil.

Swan

For anyone who has seen a swan then you know the feeling they bring you. I once saw seven swans fly over my head. I never knew if it was real or a vision, but I will tell you this; it brought joy and awe to my soul. They truly embody grace, love and beauty. A beautiful tale tells of a lovely girl named Caer who turns into a swan every year. Her love and Soul mate Aengus the God of Love too turns into a swan and they fly away together. This is a true vision of femininity: which is why women and swan tales have been around for a long time. One could say that the soul is feminine and the body is masculine. The swan is a symbol that captures that vision well (Carr-Gomm, Page 70-72).

Wolf

It is unfortunate how the wolf has been viewed, but here we will embrace its true worth and beauty. In my humble opinion the wolf is nothing more than a wild dog. Though it is an animal that can live alone and be comfortable; know that when it mates it mates for life. Being faithful is a strong wolf trait and they do contain great inner strength. Anyone should be honored to have the wolf as their totem, power animal or spirit guide.

It does have similar traits like that of the dog, but like the fox this is a wild animal and it thrives on that wildness. However, if integrated into cross breeding of the dogs and the wolves, which they often did… this changed things some, but they were highly prized animals (this mixed breed) and was often used during battles. Like the bear and other animals the wolf's teeth and claws were used as amulets and their hides for protection from "epilepsy".

Many Scottish clans used the wolf as their clan totem. There are stories that said that even Merlin found solace in the companionship of a wolf. It will always be a great animal ally for anyone who wishes to work with this faithful guide (Carr-Gomm, Page 76).This concludes this section for the Druid viewpoints and philosophies regarding Animal Spirit Guides. You may have realized that they use many of these words interchangeably. I do feel that these people and the Celtic peoples had good times telling stories and yes, they did enjoy hunting. It was part of their way of life, however, for the most part many of these people knew that they could not do too much to disrupt the balance in the natural order of things.

Animal Totems

So while we began by discussing Chinese Astrology and those respective animals, we are now going to discuss Animal Totems as pertains to Shamanic and Native American traditions. For me, I probably use this term the most. Similar to that of the Chinese system the Native system to the Americas centered around the seasons. They too had an animal, but instead for every year, the standard is one main animal for every month. Similar, also there are "hidden" animals and "secret" animals also, which is comparative to some of the Chinese theories also.

To give an example: I was born in the middle of June. The animal that is assigned to this time is Deer. Before I even knew that the deer was my Totem, I loved deer and had a close connection with them. Having been raised around many Native peoples I had grown interested in not only their philosophies but also their ideas on animals and what their purposes are.

Similar, though too, like the Celtic peoples they had such a deep reverence for their animals that in many cases they modeled themselves after them. In addition, they also used all parts of the animal. They wanted nothing to go to waste. An important example of this would be the Buffalo. There was no part of this animal that was wasted. It is no wonder they became enraged when the Buffalo hunters came along; not only killing their food but wasting the meat and not conserving or using it appropriately.

There is a season, a reason, and a meaning for everything that is happening in our beautiful world. Native peoples to the Americas have over history noted this Worlds worth. The Earth, our Mother: they knew and regarded her true worth and they were unfortunately eventually considered to be "heathen" in nature and much of their way was lost to the greed of the men of that time. Has anything really changed? For those people, it changed everything. They were used to hunting and Gathering as their way of life. They were then, many of these people forced to become farmers, and this was something many of them struggled with. Their way of life changed and so did the way of life for the many animals that they depended on for food, clothing and shelter.

Their beliefs though, for those who did not allow another culture to change them, many of them kept them intact. There are not as many Elder's any more as many of these beautiful people have passed on. So, keep in mind that Native American peoples followed the cycles of the moon. They followed these cycles not just as a way to keep track of the seasons; it was really to remind themselves of Great Spirit and the many blessings that were often offered to the people.

So to begin there was a cycle and this cycle was named after certain Moons. It goes as follows: This is re formatted but all information was retrieved from www.crystal-cure.com; Stones by Emily.

Rest and Cleansing Moon—January 20-February 18—Otter

Big Winds Moon—February 19-March 20—Wolf

Budding Trees Moon—March 21-April 19—Falcon

Frogs Return Moon-April 20-May 20—Beaver

Corn Planting Moon-May 21—June 20—Deer

Strong Sun Moon-June 21—July 21—Woodpecker

Ripe Berries Moon—July 22-August 21—Sturgeon

Harvest Moon—August 22—September 21—Brown Bear

Ducks Fly Moon—September 22-October 22—Raven

Freeze up Moon—October 23-November 22--Snake

Long Snows Moon—November 23-December 21—Owl

Earth Re-newel Moon—December 22-January 19—Snow Goose

According to Stephen Farmer of *Earth Magic* in Chapter 9 he discusses Animal Spirit Guides and Totems in depth. He, like me, uses many of these words interchangeably as do many other people. But I remember when I was young and traveled with my grandmother to a Reservation. I remember they had a Totem Pole. I remember that day and was so small and looking up at that pole and was really in awe of its size and the depth of the details etched in the animals faces.

So, just like before I will, this time give the twelve animals and their meanings. I will go a step further here and give my own interpretation of these animals. I am familiar with most of these animals except the Sturgeon. I live in Minnesota and we have all of these animals and birds here in this fine state. I can say, other than a Brown Bear, in my case it was a Black Bear— but I have seen all of them at one time or another in the wild of my very own State.

Otter—This animal is truly adorable. Make no mistake though, they are very protective of their young. Otter reminds us to be playful and mindful of our youth. The otter is a symbol of joy and for women: Motherhood. Look at a picture of an Otter—they look like they are smiling. Playfulness is also another keyword. Otter nudges us gently to not take life so seriously; allowing our lives to unfold naturally and yet with zest. It is time: Otter says to awaken your inner child, play more and enjoy life.

Wolf—The Wolf is one of my totems and I languish to meet one! My daughter actually has played with some wolves in a Wolf Sanctuary located in Colorado. They are one of many treasured animals. In Native tradition the Wolf is usually a symbol of Intuition. This totem allows us to be closer to Spirit. What does the spirit of the Wolf teach? It teaches us to be humble and not be afraid to look inside of ourselves and face our darkest fears. Most Wolf people are extremely sincere and are loyal people. This is a true totem for someone who seeks constant knowledge and learning. The wolf is a great teacher and will bring you steady guidance and bright intuition.

Falcon—This is a true bird of Wisdom. Sometimes compared to the Hawk, but this is a bird all its own. Above all they have great agility and much grace. This is a bird of action; but only when the timing is right. Similar, to the Hawk when a Falcon is in your life, it probably has been with you for many lifetimes; it is a key connector to past-lives. This bird will lead you to the threshold of success—know when to take the plunge. Patience and perseverance are also key attributes of this totem).

Beaver –The Beaver is quite a creature. With its large teeth and its large flat tail it does command your attention. This is a busy animal. Interestingly, this animal is at the threshold of the dream world. They show us how to build our dreams up and make them into a reality. In addition, if a beaver turns up un-expectantly than it is a sign that you may soon need dental attention. The beaver can help you reach those goal and dreams that you are aspiring towards for yourself and helps you encourage others to build their own dreams as well.

Deer—The deer is my birth animal totem for the month of June in the Native American system. Similar to the Stag as mentioned in the Druid section, this animal is about peace and tranquility. The Deer stands for gentleness and Innocence. It reminds us to think about seeing ourselves in others and to remain compassionate even with those who do not share the same values. The deer also reminds us to be gentle with ourselves e find when we connect with our inner child (and that daily we should feel refreshed and awakened by our own inner peace that resides within). The Deer also stands for vulnerability and humility.

Woodpecker—The Woodpecker is loud and he does expect us to pay attention. This bird stands for Foundation and Rhythm. It can prevent us from staying in a rut and can stimulate us into a new pattern. In Native American tradition the woodpeckers sound is followed like a heart- beat or a drum beat, and it allows the Shaman to enter a different realm behind the veil, and this bird helps keep the Shaman focused while they are on their inner journey. He expects us to pay attention to our bodies "rhythm and sounds and heed what it is telling you."

Sturgeon—This is a fairly large fish. Generosity, Determination and Perseverance are good words to describe the symbolism of this great totem. It is crucial for this totem person to realize their limitations, though. These folks are prone to avoiding their heart chakras. They need to be coaxed into displaying affection. It is crucial that you learn to control impulsive behaviors and work on areas of arrogance and self-indulgence. Many Sturgeon people become teachers though and there is great Wisdom in Sturgeon medicine.

Brown Bear—I spoke of the Black Bear earlier. Most Bears have that power. It is truly not relevant in regards to the color of the animal. Often this depends on where the Bear comes from. My experience was with a Black Bear. I have never seen a Brown Bear in the wild. Being in the presence of a bear is something you will never forget. I believe if you face one in the wild and live that is surely a sign that the Bear is your totem. This animal stands for Caution, Healing and Leadership. Like a Bear that faces hibernation in the winter, so must we sometimes learn how to hibernate in our own caves of our minds. If you are guided towards a leadership role than more than likely you have Bear as your totem. A psychiatrist that I know who does my sons assessments for Autism has Bears all over his office. I asked him about it, he loves Bears. He surely is a leader too! Even people who may not believe in totems do have them, this is a truth in life I have come to accept.

Raven—This bird is similar to the Crow but it is a symbol of Healing, Magic and Creation. This bird to me speaks volumes to us. Some even have the ability to learn the human language. They are so wise. Look into the eye of a Raven—it knows your secrets! This is old medicine bird that goes back to the beginning of Creation. It teaches us to bring out the light that resides in us all—no matter how we see ourselves. The Raven can also stimulate our senses and enhance our intuition and then our intentions become much clearer to us.

Snake—The snake similar to the beliefs of Chinese Astrology is a symbol of true healing to many Native American peoples, the snake for the most part is considered a fortunate totem or protector to have. This is a symbol of Healing, like the Raven. It promotes deep wisdom and initiations. The snake is also a symbol of creativity and will allow us to awaken that Kundalini energy that resides inside each of us. The element that resides with the snake is Fire. There is no stopping the snake—he is a true symbol of eternity and transformation. The Caduceus is a symbol of healing in the present day medical world also.

Figure 4: This is the Eye of Horus and the two snakes entwined around the pole; known as the Caduceus. This is my personal drawing and interpretation of an ancient symbol of life, healing and the eye represents the eye of "GOD" that is always watching. There are other interpretations of course, but that is a topic for another book altogether.

Owl—The Wise old Owl: You have heard this term. This bird, also like the Raven stands for Magic. In addition, it stands for Omens and Wisdom and all that is Feminine. This Bird of any type of this species promotes prophecy and eternal wisdom. This is the bird that helps a true Prophet extract the secrets that belong to the Universe. The Owl person has an unfortunate ability to see the darkness inside of souls, this can be very frightening. Remember the Owl is also a Messenger, and you need to let her wisdom guide you. An old story says that if you hear an Owl hoot three times that someone close to you will die. I think it is a Harbinger, but not necessarily for Death. It is a reminder to keep our awareness and our wits about us at all times.

Snow Goose—This totem promotes Determination and Perseverance. You will succeed at all costs. This totem also helps promote strength in your community and helps to keep you stable and promotes far reaching vision. You strive for clarity and pure vision. You are very ambitious, not really for others but more for yourself.

1) www.linsdomain.com
2) http://native-american-totems.com/birth-totems
3) http://a-rainbow-of-spirituality.org/sturgeon.html

All of these descriptions have been retrieved from various cited sources. In truth, much of this is also my own interpretation. Much of this information has been around for a very long time. I have put these interpretations into my own words as much as possible. Since I am not the original writer of these methods of belief, I did look for credible sources to back up my own professional opinion. The more knowledge we have and the more read and research—the more we can educate others as well.

Just so you know, as many people know there are very few original thoughts left in the Universe: I'm sorry, but chances are if someone else's thought of it, you might have or someone else too could have had a similar idea, thought or dream. This type of information and knowledge is for everyone, you see. We all have a right to learn, teach and grow from it. Where it is needed and required I have cited Authors and others who have professional opinions on these matters.

Native Tradition in the Ojibwe Tribe is slightly different: which is what my two sons are. They are in the Turtle Clan. My friend (but also) in the same tribe my sons are with and it is in the same family, though extended: she was in The Bear Clan, instead of the Turtle clan, like my sons, in addition they are considered 4th or 5th cousins, so it is more like extended family. There are many interpretations of a simialr theme, construct and story, based on the varying tribes that once covered the Americas. There are many clans and tribes, so I am not focusing on any one too closely, as that is not the subject of this book.

In Ojibwe tradition and there were many varying clans as with any tribe: They had 21 major Animal Totem clans. There were however originally five main totems: Crane, Catfish, Loon, Bear, and Marten. I do know that my children though Ojibwe they also are Sioux and there are many confusing notions when Clans change or mix with other tribal peoples. As recorded by William Whipple Warren the 21 Totems are as follows: Crane, Catfish, Loon, Bear, Marten, Wolf, Reindeer, Merman, Pike, Lynx, Eagle, Rattlesnake, Moose, Black Duck, Sucker, Goose, Sturgeon, Whitefish, Beaver, Gull, and Hawk. You can see that birds make up a significant portion of the Native American Animal totem system.

I cannot address all Tribes, unfortunately that would take an eternity. Though, I have given these examples for you, (the reader) so that you see not only similarities, but also as a contrast so that you can see though much of it is familiar; some tribes have different viewpoints and others have similar ones http://www.magnetawanfirstnation.com).

Figure 6:

Below is another Spirit Art image by Master Spirit Artist AHONU. This is an Animal Totem Badge. The two animals reflected from above are The Falcon and The Wolf.This image is a reflection of the animals that protect this person. Regardless of where one is these animals become your protectors; your totem, your Guides.

There are eight African lions on the outside of the square. There are 24 Horses, four Wolves and 12 Falcons. It stands for Courage, Freedom, Intuition and Wisdom. This could also be called a Power Shield. It makes a lovely piece of art work: Large enough to fit on your wall or small enough to carry in your wallet. You choose the size. This is one of the greatest gifts I gave to my children. They have become empowered by these animals. This concludes this section on Animal Totems (www.AHONU.com).

Power Animals

We are now moving into the term Power Animal. Stephen Farmer has a good description of such in his book *Earth Magic* in chapter 9 as previously stated. However before we explore that, I am going to speak about the Power Animal.

Though as I have stated these terms are quite interchangeable, I feel that a totem for me is often a symbol such as maybe a Wolf tooth or a Bear's claw. This is a true connection to that animal. For me a Power Animal is partly a New Age term, but more importantly—it is about connecting with that Power that the animal is exuding. According to Stephen Farmer, he says in his book, and I quote, "A power animal is a spirit animal that is employed by a Shaman and provides, healing, guidance and protection." In truth, it is specific enough in that it states that it is acting on behalf of the request of a Shaman or Medicine Man or Woman (Farmer, Page. 78).

So, I do agree with Farmer completely when he says that statement. In addition he goes on to say that domesticated animals typically are not Power Animals, as they are more like Spirit Animal Guides. Power Animals are for the most part wild animals, not pets that we love. It must also be said, that people and Shamans who work regularly with their Power Animals have a close relationship, and in many cases become more than allies they become friends. Often, animals that were once peoples pets and have thus passed away, often become animal Spirit guides. In other cases these beings were possibly even our own ancestors coming back as animals.

Story

This story applies more to the Chinese Astrology but it is actually a really good story to show how this works. There was a man in Tibet and he had a family and a wife. One day this man noticed a very large snake in his tree outside of his home. He was scared. He watched this snake for several days, before he decided to call some monks to see what the snake wanted. When the monks arrived they went to see this snake. They consulted themselves and did some Pujas (prayers).

Finally they stopped and they turned to the man and said, "This snake was once your wife. In your last life, she died before you did. She has been searching for you as a snake. She found you here and she still grieves for you as a wife grieves for her husband." The monks did a blessing and left the man to tell his family. They began to feed the snake and they allowed it to stay and become a part of their family. This is not a Native story however it really shows the depth of what some of our previous loved ones will do to stay connected to us.

Story

Here is a story about my Wolf Power Animal. Both my daughter and myself have great reverence for this animal. I began to work with this animal once I began my Shamanic training, I just was not aware of its presence until this particular evening.

One day I asked my friend to bring her children over so that my children and hers could enjoy a play date together. When my friend arrived, and it was a cold winter evening, her son got out of the car. I was already standing on the steps, and I was waiting for them to walk up to my back door step. Her son began to stare and he was pointing at me. I could not hear what he was saying but he looked terrified. He was just pointing at me. I looked to the right and then to the left, I yelled to them with the blustery wind catching my words, "What's wrong?" Her son had stopped right in his tracks. Finally, he started to walk towards me. I asked him what was wrong when he got close enough to hear me. He said, "There was a wolf on the steps. I saw it." I looked at him and truly did not get it at first.

I said, "A wolf? Junior: you're seeing things?" My friend looked at me she made this face like do not ask again. Later I did ask again, and he said that where I was standing he saw a Wolf instead. He did not see me right away. What he saw: was A Wolf: my Power Animal. He was my friend, my steady companion and he worked with me back then daily; and still does to this present day.

So know that at any time your Power Animal can leave. Sometimes it is because they are not getting the attention that they deserve and in other cases it is time for them to move on. Often, they make or break that relationship.

I am told by My Guides that we all have 12 main animal totems. This excludes your Birth Totems based on Month, Year or Day. We also have a Shadow totem. This is a totem that I believe stays with us from the beginning of our soul's existence until the end, if there is one. In addition, we also have our power animals and we can have more than one of those too. We will be exploring that topic here, shortly. There are as I have expressed several categories in regards to Animals and their metaphysical and spiritual purposes. Now we are moving along to the next topic.

Shadow Totem

My shadow totem of all things is The Spider. This is my personal opinion on Shadow Totems and may or may not be the same opinion as other people. I think our Shadow Totems often reflect our deepest fears. Spiders have always been attracted to me. I really was fearful of them for a long time. Let's just say the bigger the fear the bigger the spider. Over time, like with my fear of bees it got out of control where then my daughter was only four months old and in fear from this tiny insect I threw her at her father, hoping he would catch her because a Bee had landed on me. There is usually tremendous fear or intense revulsion to our Shadow Totems. They often represent some aspect of our selves we do not like or will never like. In some cases they are even parts of ourselves that we fear; in essence it reflects our own shadow self.

Story

This is my story about how I discovered my Shadow totem. There were many indications leading up to meeting my Shadow Totem. Each time I was faced with a spider, it was bigger and scarier. I had several altercations with giant spiders. My first was in an apartment where a Wolf Spider made its home in my window sill. I am ashamed to admit but I did kill that one. About a year later I went to Missouri for a Vision Quest with my Shaman. I saw a very large tarantula like spider crawling on the side of the house. That one was in the wild and never bothered me at all. I was just really scared when I saw spiders, and I remember when I saw that spider; I knew that though repulsed I was fascinated at the same time.

My third altercation, and truly it was probably my last confrontation with a spider until I dealt with that very intense fear that would rise when I saw any spider. A former friend of mine had been bitten from a Brown Recluse. This bite is very deadly for some people; especially the very young and elderly folks who have weaker and under-developed immune systems. About one month after my friend was bit, I was sorting laundry and was getting ready to move to a new place. We had boxes all over the place. I stuck my hand into a pile of dirty clothes, and I saw something move. Then I really saw it: A Brown Recluse spider just like the one that had bit my friend. They have distinct markings on their back, like a violin. They are big, not hairy though. I screamed, I told my daughter to run and get my neighbor. Something then told me he would not hurt me. I looked at the spider while my daughter was frantically trying to find someone to come to our apartment. I looked into his eyes and he was looking into mine. We actually had a conversation if I remember correctly. The spider asked me not to kill it.

By the time one of my neighbors came, I had already "ordered" the spider to crawl into this children's bank that belonged to my son and it just happened to be sitting right where I could grab it. I scooped it up without touching it at all and my neighbor came in, he said, "Oh, looks like a poisonous spider." I said, "Yeah, it sure is." I then brought it outside and let it go under a tree that was in this wooded area further away from the apartment building. From that point on I could no longer kill spiders or any bug for that matter. I had a whole new insight into the world of the Spider. I shuddered, but I knew that it was my Shadow totem. It had become too obvious, really.

So not much to say about the Shadow Totem other than this totem is based on Fear and Loathing. Sometimes, it is just bugs, but other times it could be an animal like a Snake, or say a Komodo Dragon. Or it could be something like a very scary or aggressive animal such as a Panther or say a Scorpion or a Rat. So this ends this short segment on Shadow Totems. When trying to discover your Shadow totem, just find yourself thinking about what scares you, meditate on it, and it shall be revealed to you. No one needs to know either, this is private between you and your Shadow Totem. Once you accept the Shadow Totem, it will become your friend and ally. There is no longer a need to be a afraid of that species or animal any longer.

African Animals and Totems

Africa! The word is just exciting to say. I have always wanted to go see Africa. The closest I have come to that was on vacation to Lion Country Safari in California when I was nine years old. I remember that while we were in this vehicle that the lions came up to it. They began to climb on our tour vehicle. They were just curious, or so it seemed. They were not hungry and they were in a playful mood. I do see why people are mesmerized by giant cats. We forget that not all cat's play the way our pets do. There are many folks who have succumbed to the lion and that is sad, but we must try to understand. So my first African animal is the Lion: in these here parts he is King and she is Queen just like the Lion King suggests. This is not the African system, please note; these are just animals that reside in Africa that I have chosen to discuss; again twelve animals that I find to be of great importance to folks who work with totems, messengers and guides.

There is some substantial evidence that has been provided to show that Africa was the place where "mankind" was created and thus built. Many great nations have succumbed to the rise and fall of the tide of change that comes to all great lands. Africa may have hidden her secrets well, but she is starting to give them up.

Animals make up a large portion, or at least once did. Some have even referred to this magical place as "Eden." The animals sure, seem like something out of a fairy tale or a bible story. There is great ancient magic that resides under the Earth of the continent Africa. So enter: The Lion.

Lion:

Though, one often sees a picture of a magnificent lion with a mane. It is the male we often see, but this is a symbol of the feminine—true feminine power. One symbol in traditional Astrology is the sign for Leo is the Lion. So if in this lifetime you are a Leo—than the Lion is surely assigned to you regardless of belief in totems or not. There has always been fear around the lion—but in addition to that it is giving you permission to roar if threatened. This is the sign of Creativity, Intuition and Imagination. This is another symbol of an animal that is viewed as a King and therefore, often Kings have used that motif as their symbol, such as Richard the "Lion Heart". It is a powerful totem. Whether you live in China, America or Africa, if this totem is yours; strength and confidence are sure to follow you the many days of your life.

Elephant

When I think of an Elephant I think of a very stoic creature. An elephant is Noble, Strong and Proud—but not in arrogance. It is often noted that the elephant is a symbol of royalty. This is also about ancient power and resilience and strength. One of my favorite Elephant symbols is Ganesh. This is the Hindu God of Overcoming Obstacles—but our focus is the African elephant.. This too is a symbol of the feminine trinity: the Girl, the Maiden and the Crone. The Elephant totem also promotes strong family ties and motherly connections to people other than your own children. If you are born with this totem then you are probably inclined towards plant knowledge, if you have just been introduced to the elephant then it is a sign that you need to eat better food—particular herbs and vegetables. If you have an elephant you are probably a very sexually active person or have a lot of sexual energy.

Gazelle

When I think of a Gazelle it reminds me of a Deer or an Antelope, but of African descent. What a lovely graceful creature. They have speed, agility, form, and purity—with this one simple fact that they know they are prey. They are the victims of the ravages of nature, but they live on—like hope. Do not underestimate this beast. When you feel trapped this animal can help you find a way out of your dilemma. You will not remain cornered forever, and when you see your exit you make your decision and you bolt! It is a beast of action and purpose. It shows us how to prepare for the inevitable that eventually finds us all—death. It reminds us to live and feel the adventure of life! This is my own interpretation of the Gazelle. I have always secretly adored this graceful African beast! In addition, it can be an indicator when this totem comes into your life that there are times that you must remain hidden. Still, like the gazelle—follow your instinct. Look ahead of the crowd, and know when to act.

The Nile Crocodile

This ancient reptile connects us to the time of the dinosaurs, and she is the keeper of the dawn of creation. She is strong and yet she appears to be patient just waiting for the perfect moment to strike! This totem can connect you to ancient power and primal force energies. This is the symbol of true wisdom and the crocodile is the keeper of all knowledge. When the crocodile appears it is probably bringing you knew knowledge and will allow you access to great wisdom; however, do not allow that wisdom to consume your divinity. Though it allows you to touch those primal forces of nature, it also asks you to beware of unseen dangers that may be lurking in the murky depths of what remains unseen. The crocodile being a symbol of ancient wisdom is also a symbol of unbridled passions and creativity. Harness it, but unleash that power when necessary.

Cheetah

I would say that this is a totem for runners and people who are into sports and athletics. This is also an animal— if you have just been introduced—it is telling you to get into shape. The cheetah reminds us that sometimes we must run and leap for our dreams. Key words here are speed and agility and flexibility. These animals some have been clocked at 90 miles per hour. It teaches us not to over-do it, and when necessary we must rest. A cheetah person cannot handle stress, especially physical stress on the body very well. So it is important that you pay attention to your body's signals that it may be receiving while being physically active.

This totem can help make you more alert and aware to approaching danger. In addition, it helps when faced with opportunities: the cheetah can get you there faster. This is also (believe it or not it) a totem for the Healer. Many cheetah folks are also prone to suffering but I will tell you when it comes time for the suffering to end, and all the tears are dry—the cheetah is the one whose back you will ride on and speed towards success!

Hippopotamus

This animal has always been intriguing to me, similar to a hairless cow that loves to be in the water—but somewhat pig or boar like. Make no mistake—the hippo is a totem not to be challenged or messed with. Before I look up other resources I often give my interpretation before I do a reading or other types of work that require some research. My first instinct here is to say that a Hippo is full of power. This animal loves the water and this is a symbol of life, birth and eternity. It if provoked will attack only to preserve itself. Now on "Lin's Domain" as I am now turning back to this awesome resource: her keyword here is: POWER. She also states that this is the animal that is connected to the feminine connecting us to the birthing realm. They live in water and water is the symbol of life and awakening our higher selves. For people who are extremely creative and this energy flows through you this is probably your totem. Learn how to link the spiritual, the creative, heart and the mind—you link these four things together and you form a diamond.

Hyena

When I see a Hyena I think of safety in numbers. In addition I see that these animals though appear to be laughing, they are actually similar for me to compare to a Coyote. I feel that this is the Trickster of the African animal kingdom. I also feel that they are somewhat neutral…they go where the smell of food or (opportunity) takes them. Like all scavengers, they are prone to aggression when hungry. Do you know any hyenas personally? In addition, Hyenas are family orientated and they take care of their young pups; the mothers nursing them until 12-18 months. This is a sign that they are family orientated. To think in truth, could you trust a hyena?

This is the totem of "Instinct and Discernment". Hyenas are also very vocal animals, so they are associated with communication and in truth folks who have this totem need to watch what they say so that their words do not hurt others. These folks are task orientated but they like to work in a group. Hyena people just have this knowing about others; who is good for them or not; they just seem to read people very well.

Leopard/Panther

This animal exudes power and mystery. Male or female they walk with pure confidence. They are beauty incarnate. However, even though they are power: for us humans they ask us to reclaim ours, and like their "royal" birthright suggests— this is what Leopard asks us to do. Leopards are quite resourceful: they put their kill often in trees to prevent others from taking their valuable meal. This teaches us to guard what we hold dear.

There are many Virtues that this magnificent beast holds: nobility, graceful, and have enhanced personal power. There are many words I have found to describe this beautiful animal. People who have this totem are often clairvoyant or clairaudient. They are intelligent and have an ability to blend into their environment. They prefer to be alone but they have great leadership qualities. In addition, Panther or Leopard people prefer the nighttime hours and they enjoy the time of the full moon. These people are practically fearless and they sometimes like to do risky activities.

This animal represents ancient power and if you find yourself working with the Leopard or Panther, (or maybe) it is even your Shadow Totem: it is time to start paying attention. This animal does not play nice when you ignore it. There is no turning back when introduced—face your fears head on and follow your own mystery while you hold this very large cat's tail—he will take you to places you have only dreamed.

http://www.linsdomain.com/totems/pages/panther.htm

http://www.outtoafrica.nl/animals/engleopard.html?zenden=2&subsoort_id=2&bestemming_id=1

http://www.ancientkeris.com/leopard-animal-totem-ancient-keris-aka-22.html

Giraffe

This totem is very perceptive and often has many precognitive moments. As their long neck suggests, seeing over the "horizon" is part of what this totem will enable you to do. This is really about seeing far into the distance and preparing for what may be coming.

These animals do often fall as they become prey, but they are family orientated for a while until the Giraffe, as it grows older they venture away from the group and become independent yet more solitary. I feel that this animal teaches our young to move away from the "mother." It teaches us to be more compassionate for people who are different from what people consider the norm. This includes discriminating against Gay and Lesbian persons as this would be considered a totem for them personally.

This African animal can give you the right words to say at the right time—the Giraffe helps you to hold your tongue so as not to say the wrong thing to the wrong person. It reminds us also not to gossip. The giraffe is a very balanced creature. The Giraffe has her feet grounded and planted and her long neck is in the sky—held high! She teaches us about balancing between the spirit and the flesh. Pay attention to both sides of you—body and spirit. Giraffes are subject to parasites and other internal infections—be mindful of your health. If something is not right go to the doctor. The Giraffe teaches us about precious life!

(www.linsdomain.com/giraffe)

http://en.wikipedia.org/wiki/Giraffe

Rhinoceros

Similar to the Hippo and the Crocodile this animal is similar in that is the embodiment of ancient wisdom. There appears to be a theme that is running through many of these brave courageous animals. This animal is ancient, it represents CONSERVATION. This large animal with all its size, is truly a victim to those who hunt it. It is being hunted into extinction. This animal reminds us that we are constantly taking and not always taking stock in our resources—we either take too much or refuse to use the excess. This totem: if it has come into your life it represents a need to conserve, share and grow. It is sad to say that the truest predator against the Rhino is MAN. It also teaches us about greed—and the lengths people will go to take something that does not belong to them. Be mindful of your thoughts—do not covet what does not belong to you.

Since this animal leads a solitary existence, I would say this would be a good time to get to know yourself—really find out who you are. This animal can connect to your past lives and it allows you to stimulate those memories. This is ancient wisdom like no other—connected to the time of the dinosaurs. This creature also teaches us about evolution—and adapting to changes either in our present environment or it causes us to think about the future of the world and her surrounding environments. The Rhino knows who and what he is! Trust the wisdom of your heart and allow the Rhino to put things in perspective for you.

1) (www.linsdomain.com).
2) http://en.wikipedia.org/wiki/Rhinoceros
3) http://www.outtoafrica.nl/animals/engrhino.html?zenden=2&subsoort_id=
   1&bestemming_id=1

Baboon

I only had room for twelve animals in this section. I was torn between the Wildebeest and the Baboon. As soon as I saw that there was a connection to Thoth—The Egyptian God of Knowledge I knew this was the animal for me to write about—in fact as a writer I now believe that this is one of my old totems or new; (I have been writing most of my life so -- probably old totem). The Baboon was said to be the Scribes to Thoth. That they stand in the Hall of Judgment to listen to the lamentations of the departed souls who pass through those halls. This is a sign to defend family and protect our young, to preserve old traditions and defend honor and dignity. These large apes are wise and their eyes reflect their knowledge.

 It is interesting, but the truth is I understand why the Egyptians and other cultures worshiped and modeled themselves after this amazing beast: there is something called a "takeover" where another male Baboon comes along and takes over the "harem". This is a symbol also of male dominance and control—so if you are with a man, as a woman and it is a dysfunctional relationship—consult the Baboon and allow him to take over. If you are meek this animal totem will make you strong. In addition, when you look at some of the painted faces of a Baboon it teaches us about masks—and the masks that people wear.

It teaches us about the Red Road and the Blue Road. They are a perfect balance of what is: Physical and what is Divine. The Baboon is the one who helps you speak and write your truth. Thoth—God of Knowledge and Wisdom had kept them as pets and he empowered them to speak and write. His prized Baboon—known as Babi: his name meant "Alpha Male"—for men this is your totem if you are highly charged sexually. This totem speaks to the men to be empowered by their manhood without being offensive to women. The baboon reminds us to pay attention to our emotions especially Anger: and find positive ways to cope with negative emotions.

(http://en.wikipedia.org/wiki/Babi_(mythology)

http://www.spiritwalkministry.com/spirit_guides/land_animal_spirits

Zebra

This animal looks like a black and white horse or a mule. I find it interesting that each Zebra, though may appear to be identical actually all have their own unique and distinct markings. This promotes the trait of being an individual. The Zebra can help you when it comes to climbing over obstacles.

They are so unique that if you really paid attention you would find him or her in the crowd: they stand out but blend in at the same time. This animal also teaches you about diet. I am inclined to say that this animal would be an indicator that people that are vegetarian or vegan probably have this totem at some point. They eat grass and are never far from water—drink water. Pay attention to your body, your surroundings, and your fear. Zebras have a high stakes game in the wild. They are often under attack by hyenas and lions. They have a stressful life you could say. If you have stress in your life, especially with a boss or your mate it is time to face the bully head on and tell them what you think. The Zebra has no problem defending their young, sick or weak. They are very protective of their young. It teaches us to protect our rights, our family, our friends—and the Zebra keeps us strong.

As mentioned previously, where I felt I needed to make citations I did. Much of this has become common knowledge. Though, I learned some amazing new traits also for many of the African animals that have been mentioned.

Mystical Animal's and Their Meanings

This is one of my favorite subjects; to talk about things that either have not been proven or cannot be proven or that remain a fable or disclosed by some people as: Fantasy. Who is anyone really to say that something or someone or some animal does not exist? That in and of "itself" is not logical, because we know that there are many things that though not proven simply have remained undiscovered. Legends have grown sure, but only "crazy people" believe in say Fairies, or Dragons or Unicorns. This is what I have personally been told. Is this not what many folks think about such things. Well, I hate to break it to those folks who think that way. There are a lot more people who do believe because their minds are open to receiving these messages from not only the animals we know to exist but also hearing the ones that hide behind the veil. The Human Mind can be a narrow passageway. It is up to us to make the walls or caverns of our minds greater and bigger than we have been programmed to believe. We must stretch our imaginations to the limit, because once we believe if they are real, that is when they will communicate with you.

So, this is a walk down a different path. We are going to explore the world of Mystical or Magical creatures. These animals though appearing to be fictitious are actually very real, that if not in the flesh, they are indeed in spirit. I have chosen nine of these magical animals and will give the definitions and symbolism for each, as follows:

The Gargoyle: This animal is seen as a Protector and is often displayed on the old mid-evil churches as such. Though they look angry or "evil" as some might think, they are a creature like any other. They remind me truly of giant bats, or cats with wings. Some even define them as giant Monkeys, such as displayed in *The Wizard of Oz*. Some of the most typical animals used are Lions, Dogs and other animals even such as the Rhinoceros and a Hippopotamus. This Mystical Being is more often than not associated with evil and darkness. I have chosen to embrace it as a nighttime protector. They are not evil, simply misunderstood. They protect the night, and those who are innocent are watched over if they find themselves lost in the dark. Call on the Gargoyle to find your way through the darkness. This mystical being will guide you to your destination. Perhaps that is all The Jersey Devil is; and the poor thing has simply been vilified because his appearance is somehow frightening to us as human beings. Has anyone really been killed by this so called "DEVIL". More research is sure to follow on this subject.

The Griffon: This is by far one of my most favorite of all mystical species. My son has The Griffon as his Mystical Totem. This is the Keeper and Guardian of all hidden treasures. Typically the Griffon has the body of the lion, the head of an Eagle and the tale of a Serpent. For those of you who seek a clear pathway to spiritual enlightenment, I would hold onto this animal tightly. This is also a symbol for soul mates: when a Griffon mates, it mates for life. If their mate should die, then the surviving Griffon would continue its life alone until they too died. Also, believe it or not Christians once believed in them and saw them as a symbol of balance between the spirit and flesh, (The Earthly and the Divine) (www.linsdomain.com).

The Dragon: Oh, the Dragon! I am not going to go into my personal viewpoint on Dragons. I think though, most importantly we should address an issue. Dragons have also been vilified for eons. Dragons, like people come in many colors and have been spoken of in almost every part of the world. In my opinion, and probably of others but this is based on my own experience with Dragons, and shortly I will tell you a story. Typically, Dragons are often the color of the element that they represent.

For instance, Red Dragon is Fire and stands for Mastery, Energy and Transmutation. Brown is Earth stands for Power, Potential and Wealth. Green is Water and its focus or key words are Passions, Inner Depth, and Connections. Finally, Blue is Ice and it stands for Inspiration, Insight and Vitality. The Dragon I am most connected to is the Ice Dragon. You get the idea. So the dragon is a symbol of these elements, and I do believe like many reptilian species that during the Ice Age they became extinct, and only their spirits remained (www.linsdomain.com).

Story: About a year ago, in 2012 in the Year of the Dragon, no less I had a mystical experience with a Volcano Dragon. In truth my experience happened inside of a dream, but later a very gifted psychic and dear family member came to visit and asked me a question. But first I will tell you my dream. In my dream I was inside my house I am presently living in. I noticed that in my dream the sky had grown dark. I then went to look out my window and my house then became the one I grew up in. A large; and very formidable fiery looking Dragon; that was in the form of fire and rolling thunder like that of a Volcanic Eruption would look. This Dragon approached my house, which at that point again had become my house now, again that I presently live in. The Dragon (and I watched) him land on my house, on the roof. Its tail was hanging off the side of my house and in my dream was visible as such. The next day this family member who sees behind the veil asked me why I had this Dragon perched on my roof. It looked in the window at us, she said while we were discussing my dream. So this "mystical being" was real. I could not see it but she could. She had no way of knowing my dream because she asked me about the Dragon as soon as she entered my home. I told her after she told me what she saw.

So, the Dragon is neither good nor bad. It just is. It is a part of nature. We need to acknowledge its presence when we feel it. If you are chosen by the Dragon, of any type than that is a gift for you to embrace and learn from an ancient way of life. The Dragon has earned its rank in history. It is not a bad animal; you just must remember the strength of such power can come at a price. These animals had Egos and some of them if not all could think and speak like us humans. They had their own fall to contend with, you could say. The "Heart of a Dragon" what do these words mean to you?

The Unicorn: For me the Unicorn stands for Innocence. But to go a step further we shall add Purity and the need to purify. A Unicorn can restore a broken heart or that "dark night of the soul" feeling we sometimes get. If you work with the elemental realm then this is truly a beautiful totem to take you into that realm to interact with the Fairy folk. You can call on a Unicorn to change or alter weather patterns. Think of the power of a horse alone, the Horn is sacred: and that is why there are legends that say they were hunted down into extinction for their horns. The horn contained the magic and wisdom of the Unicorn. This is what my Guides are saying. What are your dreams, visions, and aspirations; allow the Unicorn to help you reach those goals; to actualize your dreams (www.linsdomain.com).

The Mermaid: This is my second daughter's favorite mythical creature. They are the stuff that dreams are made of. Dolphins, whales and other aquatic creatures usually surround them in dreams also. The mermaid symbolically is an idea of perfection through transformation. They provoke us to seek out the unknown and they bring the promise of what is forbidden; baring a luscious fruit, that if taken for granted will become toxic to us. I think metaphorically when you see mermaids they often are holding a mirror. This mirror is a symbol of our reflection; inner and outer; it is a symbol of our personal truth. Is our beauty on the inside the same as on the outside? It teaches us about vanity and not to take our looks too seriously. This is my personal interpretation of this mythical beauteous creature. It teaches us about the lessons of our youth, as well as the way we perceive ourselves as we begin to grow old in the future.

A Naga: What is a Naga? This is a snake like being, that often is part serpent and part human in nature. A Naga is a male and the Nagi or Nagini is the female word. This is a Sanskrit word for Snake. Often: referred to as being "Hooded" or "Cobra" like. They are not evil, by nature but they can cause mischief. In certain Buddhist countries they are sometimes compared to the Dragon, but more like a Water Serpent. There are many stories and tales about Naga's and their involvement with Buddha's. In India a Naga is basically a Nature Spirit, however their focus is water; rivers, wells and springs. This Being can not only promote rain to come in desolate places but many believe they are also behind floods, and other natural disasters that involve water (http://en.wikipedia.org/wiki/N%C4%81ga).

The Phoenix: This is another of my favorite Mystical Creatures. It is the symbol of resurrection, and the renewing of energies. This is truly about transforming negative elements into positive ones. This is to me a symbol of hope and triumph. This Creature is an aspect of the Sun. The legend says that it dies every night only to be reborn again with the coming of the new day at the set of Dawn. My daughter claims she saw one in a forest by our old apartment. She described what she saw to me, and I would say, she was only six years old at the time and I had never discussed this bird creature with her. I think she saw one, if only with her third-eye vision. But what a beautiful sight to behold!

Pegasus: This is a totem of Inspiration and soaring on the wings of confidence. Be inspired by the MUSE that you are. This totem teaches us about humility and being confident without arrogance. (I have to put this side note in: I just looked it up and it says that Muses worked with the Pegasus and they are the Horse of the Poet) you can read this at (www.linsdomain.com). So, no joke, they work directly with the Muses. See, the Mythology section in this book for more information.

The Centaur: I chose the Centaur on a whim. Originally I was going to do seven animals, but I chose nine instead. This Magnificent creature and Pegasus were the last two I decided to write about. The Centaur commands respect for nature and the wilderness and he is a symbol of Strength in the face of adversity. Centaurs teach us about self-control especially in areas of drinking, carousing and other deviant sexual behaviors. They teach us that even lust has its place in the soul, but instead we will use the word DESIRE. So in terms of nature if you have observed animals in the wild then you know how profound nature can be. The Centaur is a true symbol of the wildness of the "animal" that lives inside each of us. Embrace your wildness and transform yourself into an impeccable soul who understands moderation in all things (http://en.wikipedia.org/wiki/Chiron).

Animals in Mythology

I loved Mythology in tenth grade. It was mandatory at the High School I was going to and I enjoyed this class, probably too much. There are many Mythology stories regarding animals and of course the last lengthy section, (mythological animals). There is much speculation as to where these strange beasts came from; whether they were created by Source, or by Extra Terrestrials, or they were merely animals whose lives were cut short by extinction and the effects of evolution and time. I have my own theories and so we shall leave that discussion for now. I am not going to touch on every myth revolving around every animal, whether real or mystical. I will be touching on some of the high lights of stories I enjoyed from my youth.

The Myth of Pegasus

The myth behind the Pegasus is that this creature was born from the blood of the Gorgon Medusa whom Perseus killed. It is also described in Edith Hamilton's book: *Mythology* that when his hoof struck the ground that Hippocrene which would be the beloved Spring of the Poets—was sprung, this on the Muses mountain known as Helicon (Hamilton, Page. 185-186).

Athena, the Goddess of Arts, Crafts and the Counsel of War—she favored this man who longed to tame the enchanting winged steed. His name was Bellerophon and he gratefully accepted Athena's intervention and soon the steed succumbed to the charms of the Goddess and became Bellerophon's trustworthy companion. In truth, many trials were ahead of this man, and he soon would rely on the strength of Pegasus more and more. The biggest task before him was to slay the dreadful creature that caused fear in all: the Chimaera. This animal was a lion, goat serpent combination. He was able to use Pegasus to get close enough to shoot arrows into its heart and kill it. Unfortunately, all ego's bring some type of downfall. Bellerophon was no exception. He thought he could ride the steed all the way to Mount Olympus. Pegasus having known this task was impossible, threw Bellerophon off his back and he was forced to wander the Earth alone bereft and angry and hated by the Gods (Hamilton, Page.189-190).

Oedipus and the Sphinx

The story of Oedipus is one of several great Greek Tragedies. The father of Oedipus was King Laius and his birth mother was Jocasta. Before the child was ever born there was a prophecy: foretold by the Oracle of Delphi—that his child that was to be born would one day kill him. So instead, and with the help of his Mother, they fastened the infant's ankles and hands together with pins and left him on a mountain to die. Eventually someone found the wailing infant and he was adopted. He later on grew up like any lad, and began to search for his true roots. There was a frightful creature that was harassing many towns in the area. The Sphinx: had a head and bust of a woman, the wings of an Eagle and the body of a Lion. She was terrorizing these villages and people and she would stop them and demand that they answer her riddles, lest she devour them.

Finally, one day Oedipus, who had already fulfilled the prophecy and had killed his Father who had appeared to him as a simple stranger among other robbers, and he along with four others killed him (unbeknownst to him he had killed his father). He was on his own road to ruin because another Delphic Oracle had told him he would one day kill his father, which he thought was the man that raised him King Polybus—he did not know the truth about his sad past. He decided to try and find the Sphinx, and since he had no friends or family he did not care of the outcome. The Sphinx was waiting for him as he passed its usual landmark. The Sphinx asked him then, "What creature goes on four feet in the morning, on two at noonday, and three in the evening?" Oedipus responded with, "A babe creeps on the hands, a man walks erect in mid- life, and in old age, he walks with a cane. This is your answer." The Sphinx then killed herself and the land was freed from her terror. After the prophecy of the Oracle was fulfilled and the sad predictions of his life came true: He later blinded himself so that he could not "see" the evidence of his sin—the children he had had with his very own mother—Jocasta (Hamilton, Page: 375-382).

Daniel in the Lion's Den

This is a Bible Story. So, for those who do not like Bible stories, I apologize but this is a crucial one to point out the support of an animal totem in one's life. According to legend and history in the time of King Darius who was the father of the future Persian ruler—Xerxes. King Darius ruled one day that no one could pray to any God or other Deity except for him for a series of thirty days. Daniel, however continued to pray to his god and he was thus thrown into prison in a cell full of lions. I would say though there is some mythology here, more than likely this even really did occur. What would standing up to a lion mean to you? Or in Daniels case many lions? Again, this shows great Courage in the face of adversity. Speaking now back towards the signs of totems: (and Christian analogy aside), this was Daniels Totem and or possibly his Shadow Totem. The message is about facing your fears and embracing those fears. It could be seen also as a sign of standing up to unwelcome and tyrannical rules; as was the time period that Daniel lived in. He was as brave as any lion, how could they possibly kill him, he was more like a brother to them.

Jonah and the Whale

His is another Biblical tale. According to the tale Jonah was a prophet from 8th Century B.C who lived in the northern kingdom of Israel. When events used to happen to people sometimes they did exaggerate those events through story telling. I feel that the fish is often a symbol of enlightenment. I think being swallowed by this giant fish or whale is an indication that you need true vision and Divine intervention. In essence it is like being swallowed by GOD or Creator. I also think that like a whale we are being called to explore our inner depths, as

Jonah was asked to do when he was swallowed and had to explore those inner depths of the whale. He had nothing to do but wait to see if he would live through the ordeal. It teaches us to be grateful for each day that we have to live.

Krishna and Kaylia

Kaylia is one of the Naga Kings in Hindu mythology. The enemy of Kaylia was the Giant Garuda king, which was a Giant Eagle. One day Krishna—a great Lord jumped into a river to retrieve a ball. The Naga King quite disturbed by the ruckus and all the noise got angry and he wrapped himself around Lord Krishna and began to tighten his grip to kill him. Lord Krishna was so great he began to grow and expand with all his mighty strength. He then put the weight of the entire universe on the Naga kings head and he started to crush him. At that moment all of the Naga king's wives pleaded with Krishna to not kill him. As the Naga king's life ebbed Krishna decided to free him from death and permitted him to live. Naga's were known as Chiefs, and there were many. Some of this is also later interpreted as a "snake or serpent cult." Remember the snake is one of the oldest symbols of life, healing, and magic. I think a healthy dose of respect should be reserved for the snake (http://en.wikipedia.org/wiki/Kaliya).

Romulus and Remus

This story again comes from ancient Greece. There were once twin brothers: one named Romulus and one named Remus. Their birth mother was Rhea Silvia and she was then betrothed to King of Alba Longa. Amulius who was her Uncle then seizes power before the two babies were even conceived. Amulius then orders her to become a Vestal Virgin—which is a life sworn to chastity. She is later impregnated by the God Ares or in other stories the Demi-God Hercules. Her Uncle finds out and has them removed from her arms and put into a river. Similar to that of the Moses story, these babies live through a series of events that would be considered a miracle for their survival.

They land on the banks of the river and along comes a she-wolf whose name is Lupa. She then takes them as her own pups and she nurses them into childhood. While she suckles them, a woodpecker feeds them other food as they grow. In theory, I would say they were about five years old when they were found by a couple: a shepherd and his wife. They raised them into adulthood, and still unbeknownst to them they lived their lives as simple shepherds tending to their foster parents flock. They eventually discover their origins and they kill their Uncle Amulius. Instead of waiting for their rightful inheritance, they decide to go out and build their own city. It is said that this great city was formed by the death of Remus. Before this event however, the twins decided to consult an augury which was a special priest who determined events through studying the flight patterns of birds.

Both of these young men are fighting now over the same space. Remus uses the number six to describe his power and the Vulture was his bird. Romulus, chides him and says he has twelve birds and they are Eagles. Then, Remus counter challenges and states, that he saw his birds first. Well, of course, Romulus ignores his brother and continues to build on the spot that they both desired to have. Remus then, enraged and insulted leaps over the wall only to be met by a blow to the head by his brother. This is similar to the Cain and Abel story. There were three main animal messengers in this tale: The Wolf, The Vulture and The Eagle. The Eagle later on became one of the symbols of Rome and was historically dating back to its founding in April 21 753 A.D (http://en.wikipedia.org/wiki/Romulus_and_Remus).

Athena and the Owl

For anyone who knows about Greek Mythology; you most certainly have heard stories about Athena and her Owl. The Owl as stated before is a true symbol of Wisdom. Her Owl was named Glaucus. Though, it was doubtful this was a pet but more like a manifestation of her in the form of a bird. It is speculated that people think that wisdom is reflected in the eyes of the Owl which is what makes their eyes glow with that inner fire. This is truly how "we" thought back then, and so it is a true symbol of ancient wisdom given to us by the Goddess herself. Athena is said to be in the 5th Ray of light. She like the Owl promotes us to speak our truth and keep secrets hidden that should not be revealed. The 5th Chakra has to with speaking, writing and communication. Therefore, it also promotes speaking ones truth and seeking out the truth in all things. Athena is considered one of the Wise Masters—she and her owl represent that ancient wisdom. If you are not motivated, Athena and her owl will do just that you. There is no time for procrastination when she is present (Virtue, Page.).

The Frog Prince

There are many stories that have conveyed the plight of the Frog Prince. According to the story in *The Druid Animal Oracle* the authors speak of The Frog Prince, for those who want a more modern rendition you could watch *Shrek.* In a story from the West Isles of Scotland there was a Queen who had three daughters. She told them to fetch water, but each time they were horrified by a grotesque creature known as a Frog or a Toad in other similar stories. Each time the Frog denied them access to the well unless one of them agreed to marry him. Finally, the youngest daughter did relent and she agreed to marry him, after her mother was healed from a previous ailment. The Frog then continued to croak at her until she was compelled to strike him or in other stories kiss him. He then miraculously turns into a Prince; whatever spell was thus broken through her actions. The Frog (through her quick actions) was transformed back into his authentic and beautiful self (Carr-Gomm, Page. 64-65).

Caer: The Swan Girl

I mentioned this tale slightly earlier. I had a vision that prompted me to wonder more about the Swan. When I spoke of seeing all those Swans, I never knew if it was a vision or real, simply because it happened in February—not at a time when Swans would be soaring in the sky. This is a story of soul mates. The Swan was mentioned in other stories as in the case with Leda and the Swan (Zeus).

However, my focus here is the Celtic Story of the love that Aengus—God of Love had for his soul mate. It is said that Aengus lived among the Fairy Folk, he began his work in the art of love by his own encounter with his own soul mate a girl named: Caer. He first saw this beautiful lady in a dream, and with that he had his fill of his desire for her and he went in search of this beautiful creature. When he found her she was chained to many beautiful swans. He then, in his power and his love for her he transformed himself into a Swan and he rescued his beautiful maiden. They then, as legend says lived happily ever after every year around the same time they both turn into swans. This story is a positive take on the Zeus and Leda story—instead of it being about Lust the story it later became about Love (Virtue, Page 5-6).

The Bee Motif

I decided to end this section with the wonderful aero-dynamic Bee. The bee is really pretty amazing and resilient. I think this is a true sign of perseverance and preservation of family and community. In the 1700's Napoleon Bonaparte adopted this insect as his personal motif and symbol. The bee is truly a model for civilized society, which I think ultimately is what Napoleon in the beginning was striving for. It stands as a symbol of equals under one leader (O'Connel et al, Page 196).

In addition, there are many great things to say about the bee. Many cultures marvel at this amazing creature. Bees are not only associated with nourishment but also with the sun—therefore light. In Egypt, they were also a symbol of the sun as a symbol of the tears of the Sun god Ra. In Celtic belief honey is a key ingredient in their drink called Mead—it was considered an elixir of the Gods (O'Connell et al, Page 197).

To conclude this section, I hope that you have seen a storyteller's perspective on some of these animals that were either introduced earlier in this text or are now being mentioned presently. These animals are here to inspire and the stories are here, old and new to teach us lessons about their respective and in some cases; secular wisdom.

Learning your Personal Animal Totems

There are many ways to learn what your totems, guides, protectors and power animals. I think one of the best ways is to truly think about what animals you have seen in the wild, what animals are moving you in your spirit and what animals speak to you in dreams, if any.

I am not a pronounced Shaman, meaning I was never made one in ritual by my Shaman, but in spirit I am a Shaman. I am Wise and I am in the knowing. I practice many aspects of Shamanism, and here I will call myself one, but again, it is a title—and at the end of the day I am still: ME. We all can be these things, but we must remove fears. We must acknowledge the natural world and the creatures that live within it. I suggest you take time, if you have no connections with nature or animals and reflect on why that may or may not be the case.

Allow the animals to come to you. Allow your worries to leave. However, you wish to meditate you can do that. You begin by speaking to these animals that visit you either physically in nature or in your dreams or mediations. As you speak to them, they will listen. If at any point you feel an animal or hear an animal communicating with you, then you need to take the time to listen.

One way to learn your totems is if you are into Dowsing. If you do not know what that is then please see my e-book on Dowsing and read it. It is an easy way to learn what your animals may be. You simply use a pendulum to retrieve information in regards to your animals. Another way to find out is by getting a reading as to what your animals are, which we will go into shortly.

Here is a quick reminder of what was said earlier: Birth Totems are based on year and or month, dependent on what idea of beliefs you follow as mentioned above.

You can follow both the Native American way and the Chinese Astrology—both of these philosophies can be quite helpful to understand some of your animals.

Also any combination of animals no matter what part of the world they come from can be interchangeable, or in truth, see how many animals you actually can identify with and relate to. Look at it this way, there would be more helpers with their own perfect wisdom to guide you. In addition, and this is simply what my guides have told me you must trust your own instinct sometimes on this subject. There are twelve months in a year (and twelve is a sacred number) there are twelve animals, similar to that of the Zodiac system.

Now, in truth, these animals change for each person. To compare, we have Guides and Angels and Ancestors guarding over us: these animals can at times change with us in the same manner. We also as I have noted have a Shadow Totem and we have Power Animals. So with these different concepts there are several ways to learn about them; it ultimately is up to you to take action to get to know your animal protectors, friends, and guardians.

Let's say that you are on the beach and you spot a dolphin in the distance. Let's say then, and this happened to me, the dolphin comes closer. I was afraid of water then, and still I cannot swim, all these years later. However, the dolphin he was meant for me. I even have a photo of him as he flips his fin at me as he departs. I had my then oldest daughter on my hip, as a baby. We waved at the dolphin and I will not forget that experience. Now, though that is not one of my main totems but was simply a dolphin messenger for me to give me a sign that I needed to play more and pay attention to my breathing. I was very out of shape at that time. The dolphin encouraged me to take care of myself better and I did have much more joy in my life after that point.

Establishing a Relationship with Your Totems

Like any friendship it is important that you communicate with your animal spirit guides and guardians. They are not only your friends they are your teachers. They have many lessons to bring to us. Many Guardians and Power Animals go on alone when their designated "charge" ignores them. I have even had such experiences myself. Sometimes, also an animal will come along to teach you a lesson that is only temporary; meaning if a turtle crosses your path while you are driving, it teaches you about patience. I have seen plenty of people, sadly run a turtle over because they simply lack the patience for it to cross the street.

In Stephen Farmers book, *Earth Magic* he discusses ways to bond with your animal protector or guide. There are several ways: visually, through auditory means, through feeling and through your thoughts. You will find the technique that works for you.

So, visually—when you see an animal or have an interaction with one or more you must either journal about it or take mental notes. What do you see or envision, that the animal could help you with? Now remember that not all visions are what manifest in real life. Some visions are acquired through dreams as I have previously mentioned. Other people literally have visions of animals helping them; whether it is through your eyes, your third-eye vision, or through your mind visualizing—this is one way that you can begin to establish a relationship with one or more of your animal guardians or protectors.

Secondly, as Farmer suggests when you hear the sound of an animal or a bird you will also see this as a sign, (through auditory means) that an animal is communicating a message to you. For me, I have many animals now that I feed and they often wake me before dawn in little ways to tell me they are waiting for their breakfast. I have many animals such as Squirrels, Crows, Wrens and Sparrows, Ducks, chipmunks, and sometimes foxes and coyotes come. I do not see them all as my totems but often just as sweet little messengers who are grateful for food and conversation. Yes, speak to the animals and they will bring you little gifts. I once saw a crow drop a marble into my sons Dad's hand. Every day we talk to the creatures and birds that come to my home. They watch over us and I see them all as my family's helpers (Farmer, Page 81-82).

Thirdly, there is feeling. We have our many senses, and touch and through empathic interpretations you can sense and communicate with your designated animal protectors. Often we have gut feelings and intuition can helps us to feel our animals around us (Farmer, Page. 81-82).

As stated to me by Aingeal Rose O'Grady: Akashic Records Reader and Writer: "sometimes we just know". To be in the knowing is a powerful thing. It does not matter if you perceive yourself as psychic or not: this is one way that your animal can get through to you without you even knowing. You just will have an" inkling" about something, and it then becomes instinctual, and you follow that pattern or message willingly because it is a part of your deep inner thought processing. To be in the knowing is a simple cognitive state. We are thinking, we are thought. If you are prone to analytical thinking over any other type then this is a good way for you to connect with your spirit animals. Sometimes we just have these "ah-ha" moments. This can happen to us when our animals are trying to communicate with us, but we are more materialistic in our thinking and cannot quite grasp the metaphysical.

So, my best advice, as sound as I can give—if you want to get to know your animal guides and protectors besides the ones that are assigned to you at birth: You need to talk to them and find ways to communicate with them and let them know you are listening. Otherwise, like all good things, that relationship will either come to an end, or will not even reach fruition. It is your job to keep the candle burning in the window, so to speak. You are the one they are seeking; if you ignore them they will not be there for you when you need them the most. If you are studying Shamanism, or just wish to know what your totems or guardians are—then this is a crucial part of the understanding. To know them you must love them and trust them and believe that they are real: then all else seems to fall into place.

Animal Totem Readings

Many people wish to know what their animal totems are but they are often too afraid to ask; mostly, because they are afraid of judgment. They think, "Oh, what will people think if I believe that animal totems are real." My two cents: Who cares what anyone thinks. Animals are crucial to our survival. They help us in so many ways that to exclude them as being meaningful is a disgrace to all life everywhere.

So, an animal Totem reading consists of a few levels. When I do a reading I first try to find out what are their present connections to any animals, past connections, fearful connections and joyful ones. I start with the day and month and year that a person was born. I use cards, dowsing, and channeling. This is done to see if any animals wish to communicate to the person receiving the reading or to me the facilitator of the reading.

So, as I stated I am told by my Guides specifically that there are 12 typical animals assigned to any one person. There is a 13th animal that is a Protector animal—like a Power animal and finally there is a 14th animal that is known as ones Shadow Totem. This reading does not include your Chinese Zodiac animal sign nor does it include the ideas based on the Native American Moon system. These are separate animals from those.

Different phases of our lives call for different animals to enter and for other animals to leave. Messenger animals are also not typically included in the reading—they are just messengers that give us temporary things to think about instead of long term ones.

To find out more about an Animal Totem reading you may go to my website for a full viewing of the link to this type of reading.

The link is: www.freewebs.com/pathwaystowellness

Other Information and Resources

In addition to a reading there are other ways to connect or relate to your animals that are assigned to you or that you may have adopted. You may seek out crafts, or art that has your animal totems etched on it or painted. There are many ways to show what your totems are. You could wear a pendant made from glass stone or a semi- precious stone shaped like one of your animals to continually connect in spirit with the animal that you feel connected to.

There are other ways to connect as well. You could make art or crafts if you are a creative person, as I have done to remind myself of their eternal presence. I make pendulums and Animal Totem tassels that are each unique and have a charm or pendant to express the meaning of the animal. There are also many resources for people who wish to know even more.

Here is a list of websites I have used and other information for the reader:

Public Domain: information on Animals and Totem meanings

www.linsdomain.com

Chantal Cash's website:

www.freewebs.com/pathwaystowellness

Spirit Artist AHONU:

www.Ahonu.com

Join the Akashic Records group online on Sundays:

www.aingealrose.com

www.worldofempowerment.com

For those who are interested in fish totems and other aquatic species and their meanings:

http://www.spiritwalkministry.com/spirit_guides/water_animal_spirits

Information on Birth Totems:

http://crystal-cure.com/article-birth-totem.html

Information on the Ojibwa people:

(My sons are half Ojibwa. This information is strictly

personal on behalf of them. Anyone else who is interested

in any of the clan information there are many websites out

there.)

http://www.magnetawanfirstnation.com/

To browse at your convenience to look up any of the mentioned animals or other creatures: real or mystical:

www.wikipedia.org

(Wikipedia is not often a reliable source, so when you read information always look for a secondary source to back it up. I still use this though for easy access to information. Much of it is reliable and accurate).

The above references are tools that I used or accessed to help me write this text. Since I have been working with totems for years, I will say that much of my interpretations are often similar to others who have written, (expertly I might add) articles, books and other commentaries on animals and their respective meanings and have given opinions also. As you think back on what you have read and learned I hope that not only this text but all those tools and books I used to help write this have reached not only your mind but your heart. It is time, if you have not already done so to connect with your Spirit Animal Guides, your Protectors and your Totem or Power Animal. Find the method that is right for you.

Conclusion

There are many aspects of the animal kingdom that we do not understand. We are in a time where animals and other species including plants and trees are facing either extinction or are being destroyed by disease, famine, fire or some other natural (or in some cases) unnatural catastrophes.

The animal Kingdom deserves to be treated as such: a kingdom in its own Divine right. We all are Divine Beings: when you see yourself inside of an animal-- meaning you can see all of creation reflected back at you in the eyes of other beings. Everything has thoughts, feelings, and impressions that may descend upon them on a daily basis. We cannot at present escape this three dimensional reality. Neither can the animals. Sometimes, even spirits are trapped here, be it human or animal or even plant life. It is time to wake up and perceive the messages what your totems, guardians and protectors are trying to tell you.

The animals have been awake for a very long time. It is we who are asleep. Yes, we are sleeping and we forgot about the reality of what once was. It has become part of the dream we all are living in. When we can all see that there are no borders, no need for control or aggression against a kingdom who has always wished to be our friends, then I think we will all know then what it is to truly be "free". When you see that and perceive that dream as a new but ancient reality— then you will truly understand what the animals have been trying to teach us all along.

One final story: When my father and my brother, and two of my four kids went out to Colorado to visit my Grandmother who I had not seen in 7 years. My dad had not seen his mother in 17 years. I knew my Dad had some health issues and my Grandmother was not getting any younger so it was a needed trip.

As we neared our destination, and on the outskirts of the Mountains I knew that there might be a chance that any one of us could see a wild animal. I was zoning out on the scenery. My Dad and brother were talking and the kids were nodding off between sleep and alert. There was no chance really for anyone to see what I then saw.

We began to round this bend, I was watching the rocks and the red hued cliffs just fly by. As we neared a sharp curve my brother slowed down the car a lot. We then were going about 15 miles per hour around this curving Mountain road. On my right side, was this very large animal. I saw as we got closer that it was a Ram, and not just any Ram—a black one with very dark spiraling horns.

As we got even closer I looked at the Ram, and I kid you not he met my gaze and followed it. We were one soul at that very moment, I felt it. Then, we were around that bend and I lost sight of the magnificent beast. I screamed, "Did you see it!" My brother quite annoyed at my question, casually asked "What?" I said, "A black Ram—Dad, did you see it?" He said, "No, I did not see anything, daughter." He called me that, when irritated.

Later when we stopped for gas before we reached my Grandmother's house we stopped at a Native American post and general store. There was an old Native man sitting on a chair on a porch whittling a bear out of a piece of wood. I approached him and said, "Sir, may I ask you a question?" He said, "Sure." I said to him then, "Can you tell me about seeing a black Ram? I saw one earlier today and he looked right at me." The man responded, but with great wisdom. "Do you know anyone who is sick?" I said "yes". He then said, "Well be prepared— someone is going to soon die." I knew that he was speaking about my father.

After eleven years I found him. He was already in end stage liver failure from alcoholism. The Ram stands for new beginnings. After my father passed away, though sad, his death opened up my life to many new ideas, perceptions, and this included stereo-typical belief patterns and negative thought forms beginning to dissolve. The Black Ram opened up my life and heart to change and allowed me not to fear what was surely coming. If anything, that Ram prepared me for it (www.linsdomain.com).

Tonight before you go to sleep, when you do your prayers or nightly rituals: I challenge you to talk out loud or in spirit to that animal that has been haunting your dreams. Or to the animal who comes to your window every morning to chatter in your ear. Yes, I challenge you to form that bond—and once you do, like me and so many others—you will never be the same person. You will see the world in a different—yet golden light. May Source bless you and your families and your pets and your ancestors—let their lights guide you back home. Let the animals, the fowl, the fish, the wild ones and our domesticated friends: Allow them to teach you the wisdom that has never died—just waiting to be relearned and rediscovered.

References:

Books

1. Carr-Gomm, Philip and Stephanie. (1994). *The Druid Animal Oracle* . Simon & Schuster, Inc.
2. Farmer, Stephen D. (2009). *Earth Magic.* Hay House, Inc.
3. Hamilton, Edith. (1942). *Mythology.* Little Brown and Company.
4. O' Connell, et al. (2007). *Dreams, Signs, and Symbols.* Anness Publishing.
5. Virtue, Doreen, Ph.D. (2003). *Archangels, & Ascended Masters.* Hay House, Inc.
6. The Holy Bible

Articles or Websites

1. www.Ahonu.com
2. www.linsdomain.com
3. www.crystal-cure.com
4. http://www.spiritwalkministry.com/spirit_guides/water_animal_spirits
5. http://www.magnetawanfirstnation.com/
6. www.wikipedia.org

7. www.chinesezodiac.com/signs
8. www.freewebs.com/pathwaystowellness

Figure 6: This is a digitally altered image of the same fox from above. It looks like a beautiful watercolor painting. This is based on the original photograph by Chantal Cash. Melaine Barnes Brown-Lee is the artist that reconditioned the photograph to look like a masterpiece of art.

Fox in Yard

4392171R00041

Made in the USA
San Bernardino, CA
18 September 2013